The Story of the Windrush

K.N. Chimbiri

golden destiny™

First published in 2018 by Golden Destiny Ltd, PO Box 65081, London, SE16 9AW, United Kingdom.

info@golden-destiny.com

Tel: +44 (0) 7980 631 077

Website address: www.goldendestiny.co.uk

Printed in Dubai.

ISBN-13: 978-0956252500

A CIP catalogue record for this book is available from the British Library.

Contents

This drawing shows a street called King Street in Kingston, Jamaica in the 1940s.

A man called Sam

In 1948, there was a young man called Sam King who lived in Jamaica, an island in the Caribbean. Sam was unhappy. The living conditions on the island were not good and there weren't many jobs available. Sam just wanted to leave.

Sam had left Jamaica before. He had travelled to England a few years earlier to help Britain during the Second World War. In those days Jamaica was a British **colony**. For hundreds of years, several European countries owned colonies all over the world. Britain had the most colonies.

*(Words in **bold** are explained in the Glossary on page 44)*

DOMINION OF CANADA
1713-1763

New Foundland
1713

North America

Bermuda Is.
1609

Gibraltar
1704

Bahama Is.
1783

Br. Honduras
1798

Jamaica
1655

Leeward Is.
1756-1784

Windward Is.
1762-1796

Barbados
1605

Trinidad
1797

Gambia
1821

Br. Guiana
1803

Sierra
Leone
1788

Western
Pacific
Islands
1877-1907

Ascension
1815

South America

St. Helena
1673

Tristan da Cunha
1815

Falkland Is.
1832

The British **Empire**. This map shows in red all the lands ruled by Britain

Europe

Asia

Tenedos
Lemnos
1915

Cyprus
1878

Bahrain Is.
1867

gypt
1882

Hinderland
of Aden
1905

Perim
1857

Sudan
1896-1899

Uganda
1895

Baluchistan
1877

Aden
1839

Somaliland
1901

East Africa
Protectorate
1895

Zanzibar
Protectorate
1896

hodesia
888-1900

ana

Transvaal Prov.
1900

Zululand
1887

Orange Free State Prov.
1900

Basutoland
1871

Natal Prov.
1842

North West
Frontier Province
1901

Socotra
1886

Laccadive Is.
1877

Seychelles
1794

India
1600-1858

Sikhim
1890

Ceylon
1796-1815

Nicobar Is.
1869

Mauritius
1810

Weihaiwei
1898

Kowloon
1860

Burma
1824-1886

Mainland of
Kowloon
1898

Hong Kong
1841

Andaman Is.
1789

Federated
Malay
States
1874-1909

Br.North Borneo
1885

Penang
1786

Malacca
1795

Singapore
1819

Br. N. Guinea
1883

Solomon Is.
1899

Western
Pacific Is.
1877 to 1907

Cocos Is.
1886

Commonwealth
of Australia
1770-1788

Fiji Is.
1874

Tasmania
1803

New Zealand
1840

show roughly when they became a part of the empire.

This drawing shows a classroom in Jamaica in the 1940s.

CHAPTER ONE
The Second World War

Many of the people who lived in these British colonies believed that England was their **'Mother Country'**. Some of Britain's colonies were in the Caribbean, which was made up of **First People** as well as people from Europe, Africa, Asia and the area called 'the Middle East'. Most people in the Caribbean were of African descent; however, in school the students were taught little about Africa or the Caribbean. Instead, the focus was on England and English history.

Because of their **devotion** to the 'Mother Country', when Britain declared war on Germany in 1939, people in the British colonies wanted to help Britain. Sam's mother said to him, 'My son, the Mother Country's at war. Go and help. If you live, it will be a good thing'.

Sam applied for a job with the Royal Air Force (RAF) in England. He passed the tests and initial training in Jamaica then travelled to England with other volunteers. After three more months of training Sam worked for the RAF in England as an engineer.

This photo shows a thousand Caribbean Royal Air Force volunteers arriving in Liverpool, England in June 1944.

Sam was just one of many men and women from all over the world who came to help Britain during the Second World War. However, after the war ended, the British government wouldn't

let Sam stay in Britain. He didn't want to go back to Jamaica but he had no choice.

This photo shows RAF Pilot Officer Ulric Leslie Look Yan from Trinidad in 1943.

CHAPTER TWO
A new opportunity

A few months after returning to Jamaica, Sam saw an advertisement in a Jamaican newspaper....

Passenger Opportunity
To United Kingdom

Troopship "EMPIRE WINDRUSH" sailing
about 23rd MAY.
Fares: – Cabin Class.....................**£48**
Troopdeck...................................**£28**
Royal Mail Lines, Limited – 8 Port Royal St.

The Daily Gleaner. Thursday, April 15, 1948.

This was Sam's chance to return to England! The ship's fare of twenty-eight pounds (£28) was not cheap. For some people this was three months' **salary**. Sam came from a family of farmers; they sold three of their cows to raise the money for him.

Sam was one of more than 500 passengers who boarded the *Empire Windrush* in Jamaica. However, Sam and the other Jamaicans were not the first Caribbean people on board the *Windrush*. The ship had already stopped at another British colony called Trinidad. Many Trinidadians also believed that England was their 'Mother Country' and they too wanted to go to Britain.

This map shows the Caribbean region. Trinidad is near the South American mainland.

Peter Dielhelnn

Peter Dielhenn, an Englishman who worked in the ship's bakery, was surprised to see hundreds of **civilians**, many of African descent, boarding the ship to go to England. He was one of the 240 **crew** who worked on the *Windrush*. When the *Windrush* first sailed from England earlier that year it had about 2,000 passengers onboard: mostly White men, nearly all soldiers from England, Scotland and Ireland. The *Windrush* was a **troopship**, carrying British soldiers to and from the colonies throughout the world. Peter thought that the ship would return to England empty apart from its crew; he didn't know that the ship would be picking up non-military passengers on the way back. 'It was really something to see', he later recalled.

The *Windrush* also stopped to pick up passengers at Tampico in Mexico and Bermuda before departing for England.

Some of the Caribbean people on board the
Windrush were of Indian descent.

At Tampico, 66 Polish people, nearly all women and children, joined the ship. During the war, they had left Poland and travelled to Mexico for their safety. Now, they too were coming to England.

On board were more than a thousand passengers from the Caribbean, Britain, Bermuda, Poland, Gibraltar, and Burma. However, it was the Caribbean people who made up the majority of the ship's passengers.

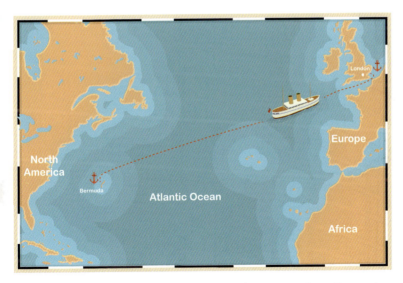

This map shows the HMT *Empire Windrush*'s journey from Bermuda to Britain.

Some people were affected by the motion of the ship, the English food served on board, or the weather.

CHAPTER THREE
The voyage

Peter Dielhenn remembered the voyage as a 'jolly occasion'. He thought that the Caribbean people were very lively. Some of the passengers did enjoy their journey from the Caribbean to England. Others hated it.

Alford Gardner from Jamaica was delighted to find that there were Trinidadians, **Barbadians** and other Caribbean nationalities on board. He found it was very easy to make friends with the other Caribbean people. He recalled, 'All you had to do was mingle'.

Some of the Trinidadians on the ship were musicians who played Calypso music. Calypso is an African-Caribbean style of music which originated in Trinidad and Tobago. It was popular all over the Caribbean. Three of the Trinidadian **calypsonians** who had boarded the *Windrush* were famous male singers called Lord Kitchener, Lord Woodbine and Lord Beginner.

On the ship, Lord Kitchener began to write a song called 'London Is The Place For Me', which would later become famous.

While some of the Caribbean people on the *Windrush* had already secured jobs in Britain, others were in the same position as Sam; they hoped to find a job after they arrived. Arthur Leigh had no money and no job, but he decided to go anyway because, 'It was an opportunity'.

George McPherson spent some of the trip working. He got a job in the ship's bakery so that he would have a bit more money when he arrived in England. He fondly remembered the journey: 'We had a fabulous time'.

One day George was working in the bakery when he heard a noise. He looked around and was shocked to find a woman in hiding. George had found a **stowaway**! She wanted to come to England too but she didn't have enough money for the fare. So she had sneaked on board and hidden herself. And now she was hungry! Many of the other passengers felt sorry for her.

Calypso music and shows like this one came to Britain before the *Windrush*.

So, they had a 'whip round'; they put together some of their own money until they collected enough to pay the captain the fare on her behalf. Now she too could legally travel to England.

Many of the Caribbean people on the *Windrush* had never been to Britain before, so Sam and the others who had been to Britain during the war told them what to expect. They explained that the country was in a bad way, the war had left London poor and scruffy, food was rationed, and the cities were bombed out. But the important thing was that there were lots of jobs available.

This photo shows office workers as they go to work after a heavy bombing raid on London.

Although most of the Caribbean passengers on the *Windrush* were men, many women and children came too. Mona Baptiste, a young Trinidadian, was one of the many Caribbean women who had helped Britain during the war. Like Sam, she decided to return and she came back on the *Windrush*.

This photo shows Mona Baptiste, a famous singer and musician from Trinidad. The Daily Gleaner newspaper in Jamaica reported on the front page that she was travelling to England onboard the *Windrush*.

CHAPTER FOUR
Starting a new life

On June 21, 1948, the *Windrush* arrived at Tilbury Docks in Essex. The following day, when the new arrivals began to disembark, the media was there. Lord Kitchener, the Trinidadian calypsonian, sang the first part of his new song, 'London Is The Place For Me' for the news cameras.

Those, who like Sam did not already have jobs, were taken in minibuses to Clapham in southwest London. There, they were housed in a collection of underground tunnels called Clapham South Deep-Level Shelter, which had been an air-raid shelter some years ago. The local people had hidden there at night for safety from the German bombs during the war.

This photo was taken in 1944. It shows children in the Clapham South Deep-Level Shelter during the Second World War.

Although Britain was still reeling from the after-effects of the war and there were lots of jobs related to the much-needed rebuilding of the country, many British people did not want to give jobs to Black people.

In colonial times some British people travelled to the colonies as **settlers**, soldiers or workers but it was not common the other way around. People from the colonies, especially non-white people, were not expected to come to Britain.

This photo was taken in 1948. It shows the Windrush arrivals, who did not yet have jobs, at a government job centre inside Clapham South Deep-Level Shelter.

Sometimes the new arrivals were paid less than White workers for doing the same job. Others often had to accept **menial** jobs below their abilities. Despite this, they didn't give up and after a month all the Windrush arrivals had a job. Some, like Sam, found work again with the RAF. Others found work with the new National Health Service (NHS). Most found jobs in London, but some found jobs in other parts of Britain.

CHAPTER FIVE
Settling down

Another big challenge for the Windrush arrivals was finding a place to live. Once they had found jobs, they had to leave Clapham South Deep-Level Shelter. But many White people didn't want to rent their rooms to Black people.

When Mr and Mrs Cecil Holness saw an advertisement for a room to rent in Tooting, South London, Mrs Holness phoned in advance to inform the landlady that she wasn't English. But when she arrived she was refused the room. The landlady didn't mind renting the room to a foreigner but she didn't want to rent to a *Black* foreigner. Many of the Windrush newcomers had a similar experience. It wasn't because they didn't have the money to pay the rent or because of anything they had done. They were refused somewhere to live simply because they were Black.

Not everyone who had sailed on the *Windrush* planned to stay in Britain permanently. Some people just wanted to work hard, make money, and then return to the Caribbean when the living conditions there improved. Others who stayed came together and tried to develop their own community. They formed their own churches so they wouldn't have to face being made to feel unwelcome in the White British Christian churches. Others used an African savings method to help each other so they didn't

need to go to the banks for money. Some managed to buy their own houses, and would then rent spare rooms to other Caribbean people.

Lord Kitchener eventually decided to return to Trinidad.

A landlady.

Allan grew up in Jamaica.

CHAPTER SIX
Before the Windrush

The *Windrush* was not the first ship to bring Caribbean people to Britain after the war.

In March 1947, the SS *Ormonde* brought more than 100 Caribbean immigrants to Liverpool. Then, in December 1947, six months before the arrival of the *Windrush*, the *Almanzora* brought around 200 Caribbean **immigrants** to Southampton. One of those on board was a young man called Allan Wilmot.

Allan came from a well-off family in Jamaica. Many of the Caribbean people who came before, and later, on the *Windrush* were well-educated, talented people.

Allan, like Sam, had served Britain during the war. Now he was returning during peacetime but things were different. People said to him, 'The war is over. What are you doing here?' He ended up, for a time, hungry, homeless and without a job.

Allan's parents were well-off.

CHAPTER SEVEN
The Windrush generation

Between 1947 and 1971 at least 300,000 people from the Caribbean came to Britain. These people are called the 'Windrush Generation', although they didn't all arrive on the *Windrush* ship. They are the **foreparents** of many of today's Black British people.

The Windrush generation came to Britain for many reasons. Some people were invited to Britain to work. Both the NHS and London Transport asked Caribbean people to come to Britain to work for them. Other people found jobs after they came to Britain. Many people wanted to work and send some money back to the Caribbean to help their families there. Some people wanted to come to Britain mainly to study.

During these years, many of the Windrush generation continued to face hardship and poor treatment from some of the White British population. Sometimes they were even physically attacked.

Yet they continued to work hard and raise their children. They worked for the RAF, London Transport, Royal Mail, and the National Health Service. They also worked in Britain's coal mines, on the railways, in show business, and in many other industries. These brave **pioneers** helped

to rebuild Britain and make it into today's modern nation. And now, people from all over the world have emigrated to Britain. By striving to improve their own lives, the Windrush pioneers changed the world.

This photo shows Caribbean people arriving in Britain on 24 October 1952.

This photo shows people in Bridgetown, Barbados in 1948 waiting for a ship to take them to Britain.

This photo was taken in Barbados in 1956. It shows London Transport inviting Caribbean people to come to Britain for work.

This photo shows an African-Caribbean man working on a steam locomotive on 17 May 1962.

This photo shows two Caribbean men reading the room 'To Let' accommodation notices in a shop window, Notting Hill Gate, 1955.

Sam B. King, MBE (1926 – 2016).

CHAPTER EIGHT
Keeping the story alive

After rejoining the RAF, Sam later worked for the postal service, Royal Mail. Then he went into politics and in 1983/84 he became the first Black mayor of the London Borough of Southwark. Together with his friend Arthur Torrington from Guyana, Sam set up a charity called the Windrush Foundation to help keep alive the story of the *Windrush*.

This photo was taken on board the *Windrush* after it arrived in London in 1948. Men from the RAF are telling the new arrivals about available jobs. *Can you spot Sam in this photo?*

The Story of the Windrush Timeline:

- **1939:** Start of the Second World War. People from the colonies help Britain to win the war.

- **1945:** End of the Second World War. Europe is left devastated. Britain needs people.

- **1947:** Two ships, the *Ormonde* and the *Almanzora*, arrive in England with hundreds of Caribbean people.

- **1948:** The British Nationality Act is passed by the British government. It confirms that people from all of Britain's colonies can come and settle in Britain. In June, the HMT *Empire Windrush* arrives at Tilbury Docks, Essex with hundreds of Caribbean men, women and children onboard.

- **1949:** The National Health Service (NHS) asks people from the Caribbean to come to Britain and work for them.

- **1956:** London Transport asks people from the Caribbean to come to Britain and work for them.

- **1958:** Violence against Black people leads to race riots in places like Notting Hill in London and in Nottingham.

- **1959:** Claudia Jones organises the first indoor Caribbean carnival in response to the race riots.

- **1962:** Commonwealth Immigrants Act limits immigration.

- **1965:** Race Relations Act is passed to address racial discrimination.

- **1971:** The Immigration Act is passed. Large-scale Caribbean immigration to Britain ends.

- **2018:** The first annual Windrush Day, a national day to celebrate the Windrush generation and their descendants.

Glossary

This glossary explains some of the words you have come across when reading about the *Windrush* journey.

Barbadian A person from the island of Barbados.

Calypsonian A singer of an African-Caribbean music called Calypso.

Civilian A person who is not in the armed forces.

Colony A geographical area that is under the political control of another country. See also Empire and Mother Country.

Crew The group of people who manage, operate and serve on a ship.

Devotion A great love or loyalty.

Emigrant A person who leaves their country and goes to settle permanently in another country. See also immigrant.

Empire A group of lands under the control of one powerful person, country or government.

First People The first people to live in an area that has been taken over by another group of people.

Foreparents Members of past generations of a family or people.

Immigrant A person who comes to a new country in order to live there permanently. See also emigrant.

Menial Work that is considered to be of low status.

Mother Country The homeland of the colonisers. See also Colony.

Pioneer A person who explores or settles in a new region.

Salary A regular payment made by an employer to an employee in return for their work.

Settlers People who create a settlement in a foreign land and move away from their homeland.

Stowaway A person who hides on a ship, aircraft or other vehicle to make the journey without paying.

Troopship A ship that transports soldiers in wartime or in peacetime.

Useful resources for parents, teachers and educators

Books:

Robin Walker, Vanika Marshall, Paula Perry and Anthony Vaughan, Black British History; Black Influences on British Culture (1948 to 2016) (2017)

Allan Wilmot, Now You Know: The Memoirs of Allan Charles Wilmot (2015)

Organisations:

The Windrush Foundation   windrushfoundation.com

Black History Walks   www.blackhistorywalks.co.uk

Credits

Illustrations by Corne-Enroc.

Book design and layout by Valeria Maria Mazzitelli.

Maps on pages 14 and 17 by Vaclav Bicha.

Map of the British Empire in 1915 on pages 6 & 7 by Anis Yusha.

Index by Jan Worrall.

Quotations on pages 9, 15, 19 and 20 are taken from the Windrush Pioneers booklet and DVD produced by the Windrush Foundation's Oral History Project.

Quotation on page 33 is from Allan Wilmot's autobiography Now You Know: The Memoirs of Allan Charles Wilmot.

Dedication

To my humble parents who like thousands of others of the inspirational Windrush generation deserve thanks for all they endured for us.

Picture credits

THE SECOND WORLD WAR

10 ©Imperial War Museum (CH 13438)
12 ©Imperial War Museum (D 15031)

THE VOYAGE

22 ©Imperial War Museum (HU 36157)
23 Trinity Mirror / Mirrorpix / Alamy Stock Photo

STARTING A NEW LIFE

26 Image supplied by London Transport Museum
27 Credit ©TopFoto

THE WINDRUSH GENERATION

36 Image supplied by the Science and Society Picture Library
37 Image supplied by London Transport Museum
38 (Top) ©TfL from the London Transport Museum collection
38 (Bottom) Image supplied by Science and Society Picture Library
39 Image supplied by London Transport Museum

KEEPING THE STORY ALIVE

41 Credit ©TopFoto

Every effort has been made to trace and acknowledge ownership
of copyright. If any rights have been omitted, the publishers offer
to rectify this in any future editions following notification.

Acknowledgements

The author would very much like to thank Tony Warner and
Darren Chetty for reading the draft and offering detailed feedback.
Their suggestions and advice resulted in a much improved text.
Thanks also to Robin Walker for a useful discussion on the number
of passengers onboard the Windrush.

Thanks also to friends and family who offered support,
encouragement and feedback: Amanda, Angel, Auntie Rose, Dee,
Deborah, Diana and Jay.

Index

Words in **bold** can be found in the Glossary. Numbers refer to pages.
Numbers in italics (e.g. *24*) are page numbers for pictures or photos.